Guess What!

Pupil's Book 2

British English

Susannah Reed with Kay Bentley
Series Editor: Lesley Koustaff

CAMBRIDGE
UNIVERSITY PRESS

Contents

Hello again!

Guess What!

1 (CD1 03) **Listen. Who's speaking?**

2 (CD1 04) **Listen, point and say.**

① Ben ② Olivia ③ David ④ Tina ⑤ Leo

3 (CD1 05) **Listen and find.**

Find Leo

Say the chant.

(sister)

This is my sister.
Her name's Olivia.
How old is she?
She's eight.

(brother)

(friend)

(friend)

 Think **Find the mistakes and say.**

Number 1. His name's Ben. He's eight.

1

Name:
David

Age:
6

2

Name:
Tina

Age:
7

3

Name:
Ben

Age:
5

4

Name:
Olivia

Age:
9

6 CD1 08 **Sing the song.**

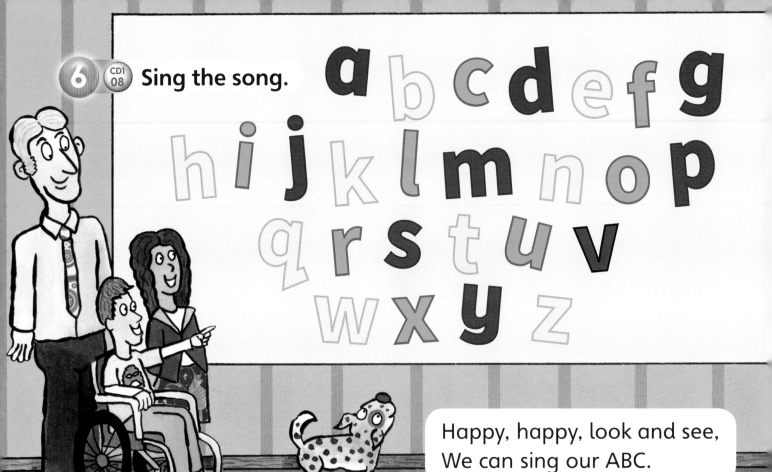

Happy, happy, look and see,
We can sing our ABC.

7 CD1 09 **Listen and point.**

Dan

Jill

Sam

Sue

Tom

8 **Ask and answer.**

What's your name?   My name's Harry.

How do you spell Harry?   It's H-A-R-R-Y.

9 CD1 11 Listen, look and say.

1 What's this?

It's a ruler.

2 What are these?

They're books.

10 CD1 12 Listen and point.

11 Ask and answer.

B, 2. What's this?   It's a red bike.

Listen and read.

Value: Play together

→ Activity Book page 8

13 CD1 15 Talk Time **Listen and act.**

Animal sounds

14 CD1 16 **Listen and say.**

The rabbit can run. The lion is lazy!

What type of **art** is it?

1 CD1 18 Listen and say.

photography   drawing   sculpture   painting

2 Watch the video.

3 Look and say the type of art.

Number 1. Sculpture.   Yes.

Guess What!

Project

4 Make a class sculpture.

① Transport

Guess What!

1 CD1 19 Listen. Who's speaking?

2 CD1 20 Listen, point and say.

1 plane

2 helicopter

3 bus

4 car

5 lorry

6 motorbike

7 train

8 boat

9 tractor

3 CD1 21 Listen and find.

Find Leo

4 CD1 22 **Say the chant.**

car

This is my car.
It's a big, red car.
This is my car,
And it goes like this.
Vroom! Vroom!

bike

train

boat

5 **Match and say.** Number 1, c . It's a tractor!

 1
 2
 3
 4

 a
 b
 c
 d

6 About Me **Ask and answer.**

Do you like motorbikes?   Yes, I do.

 **Sing the song.**

I've got a ,
You've got a 🚂 .
He's got a 🛵 ,
She's got a ✈️ .

Let's play together.
Let's share our toys.
Let's play together.
All the girls and boys.

I've got a 🧸 ,
You've got a 🪁 .
He's got a 🕯️ ,
She's got a ⚽ .

Let's play together ...

I've got a 🚁 ,
You've got a 🪁 .
He's got a 🚜 ,
And she's got a 🚲 .

Let's play together ...

8 **Listen and say the name.**   She's got a train.   May.

Tim

May

Alex

Lucy

9 CD1 27 **Listen, look and say.**

Has he got a plane?

Yes, he has.

Has she got a plane?

No, she hasn't. She's got a car.

 10 CD1 28 **Look and match. Then listen and answer.**

Number 1. Has she got a ball?   No, she hasn't.

11 **Ask and answer.**

Number 1. Has she got a ball?   No, she hasn't.

12 🔊 CD1 29 Listen and read.

1 Ben's got a helicopter!

Let's go to the park!

2 Has Ben got a robot?

No, he hasn't. It's a helicopter.

3 Can I have a turn, please?

Yes, of course!

4 Thank you. This is fun!

Be careful, iPal!

5 Sorry. Now let's play with my helicopter!

It's OK.

6 Wow! The helicopter is iPal!

Value: Take turns

→ Activity Book page 16

13   **Listen and act.**

Animal sounds

14 **Listen and say.**

A gorilla in the garden. A hippo in the house.

Where is the transport?

1 (CD1 34) **Listen and say.**

on land

on water

in the air

2 **Watch the video.**

3 **Look and say *on land*, *on water* or *in the air*.**

Number 1. On land. Yes.

Guess What!

Project

4 **Find transport on land, on water and in the air.**

on land   on water   in the air

(2) Pets

Guess What!

1 CD1 35 Listen. Who's speaking?

2 CD1 36 Listen, point and say.

1 woman

2 man

3 girl

4 cat

5 mouse

6 fish

7 boy

8 dog

9 baby

10 frog

Pet Show

Find Leo

3 CD1 37 Listen and find.

Say the chant.

mice

fish

One frog, two frogs.
Big and small.
Come on now, let's count them all.
One, two, three.
Three green frogs.

dogs

frogs

5 **Look, find and count.** I can see two women.

women

men

babies

children

6 (About Me) **Your classroom. Look and say.** I can see five boys.

→ Activity Book page 21

7 (CD1 40) **Listen, look and say.**

1
2 ugly
3 old
4 young
beautiful

5 happy
6 sad
7 big
8 small

8 (CD1 41) **Listen, find and say.**   They're cats.   They're happy.

9 **Make sentences. Say *yes* or *no*.**

Number 1. It's a bird. It's ugly.

No. It's beautiful.

10 (CD1 42) Sing the song.

I'm at the pet shop.
I'm at the pet shop.
Can you guess which is
my favourite pet?

Is it small? No, it isn't.
Is it big? Yes, it is.
Is it beautiful? No, it isn't.
Is it ugly? Yes, it is.
It's big and ugly.
Let me guess, let me
  guess – oh yes!
It's a fish! It's a fish!

I'm at the pet shop.
I'm at the pet shop.
Can you guess which
are my favourite pets?

Are they old? No, they aren't.
Are they young? Yes, they are.
Are they sad? No, they aren't.
Are they happy? Yes, they are.
They're young and happy.
Let me guess, let me guess – oh yes!
They're dogs! They're dogs!

11 (Think) Play the game.

Is it happy?   No it isn't.

Is it a dog?   Yes, it is!

Are they beautiful?   No, they aren't.

Are they spiders?   Yes, they are!

→ Activity Book page 24

Listen and act.

Animal sounds

 Listen and say.

A **f**ox with a **f**ish. A **v**ulture with **v**egetables.

What do animals need?

1 (CD1 49) Listen and say.

water   food   shelter

2 Watch the video.

3 Look and say *water*, *food* or *shelter*.

Number 1. Water.   Yes!

Guess What!

Project

4 Draw a home for a pet.

Review Units 1 and 2

1 Look and say the word. Number 1. Bus.

 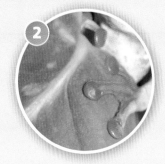  

2 CD1 50 Listen and say the colour.

Tony   Anna   May   Bill

→ Activity Book pages 28–29

3 Play the game.

What's this? / What are these?	How do you spell ...?	What has he/she got?	Is he / Are they ...?
1	2	3	4

young?

beautiful?   old?   sad?

3 Clothes

Guess What!

1 CD1 52 **Listen. Who's speaking?**

2 CD1 53 **Listen, point and say.**

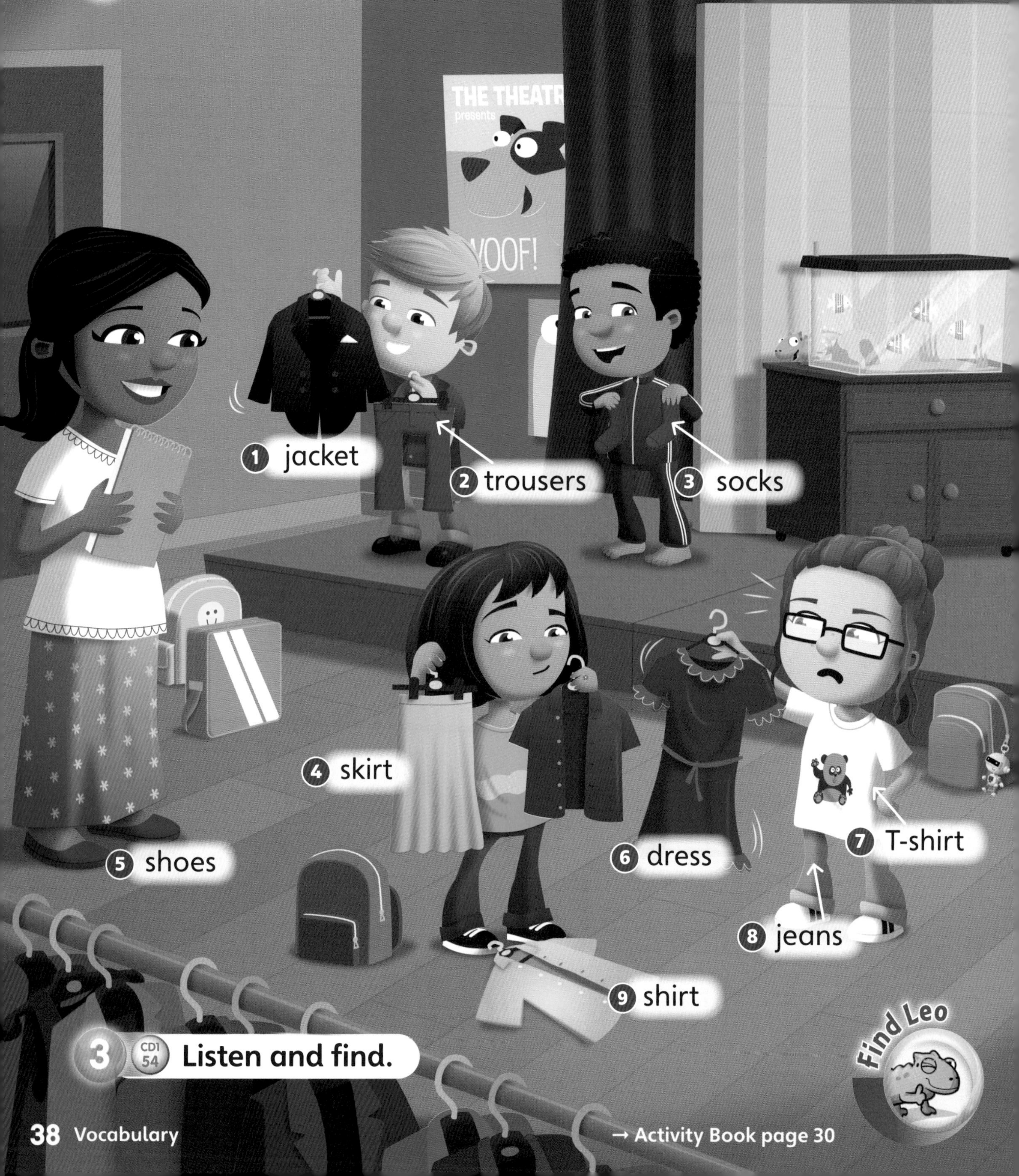

THE THEATR
presents
WOOF!
1 jacket
2 trousers
3 socks
4 skirt
5 shoes
6 dress
7 T-shirt
8 jeans
9 shirt
Find Leo

3 CD1 54 **Listen and find.**

→ Activity Book page 30

4 CD1 55 Say the chant.

red jacket

green T-shirt

purple shoes

blue trousers

Here's your jacket,
Your favourite red jacket.
Put on your jacket,
Let's go out and play.

Here are your shoes,
Your favourite purple shoes.
Put on your shoes,
Let's go out and play.

5 Think Find the mistakes and say.

His T-shirt isn't
red. It's yellow.

Her shoes aren't
orange. They're red.

6 CD1 57 **Sing the song.**

What are you wearing?
What are you wearing?
What are you wearing today?

I'm wearing red ,
And a green .
I'm wearing a blue  ,
And a yellow .
Oh! I look great today!

I'm wearing blue ,
And an orange ,
I'm wearing a green .
And a purple .
Oh! I look great today!

7 CD1 58 Think **Listen and say the name.**

Sammy   Sally

8 About Me **Ask and answer.**

What are you wearing today?   I'm wearing a blue skirt.

9 CD1 59 **Listen, look and say.**

1 Are you wearing a blue T-shirt?

Yes, I am.

2 Are you wearing brown shoes?

No, I'm not.

10 CD1 60 **Listen and point. Then play the game.**

Pink. Trousers.
Are you wearing pink trousers?

No, I'm not. My turn!

Grammar: *Are you wearing a blue T-shirt?* **41**

Listen and act.

Animal sounds

13 CD1 65 **Listen and say.**

Jackals don't like jelly. Yaks don't like yoghurt.

What are
clothes
made of?

1 (CD1 67) Listen and say.

cotton   silk   leather   wool

2 Watch the video.

3 Look and say the material.

Number 1. Wool.   Yes!

Guess What!

Project

4 Make a collage of clothes from different countries.

Clothes

→ Activity Book page 36

④ Rooms

Guess What!

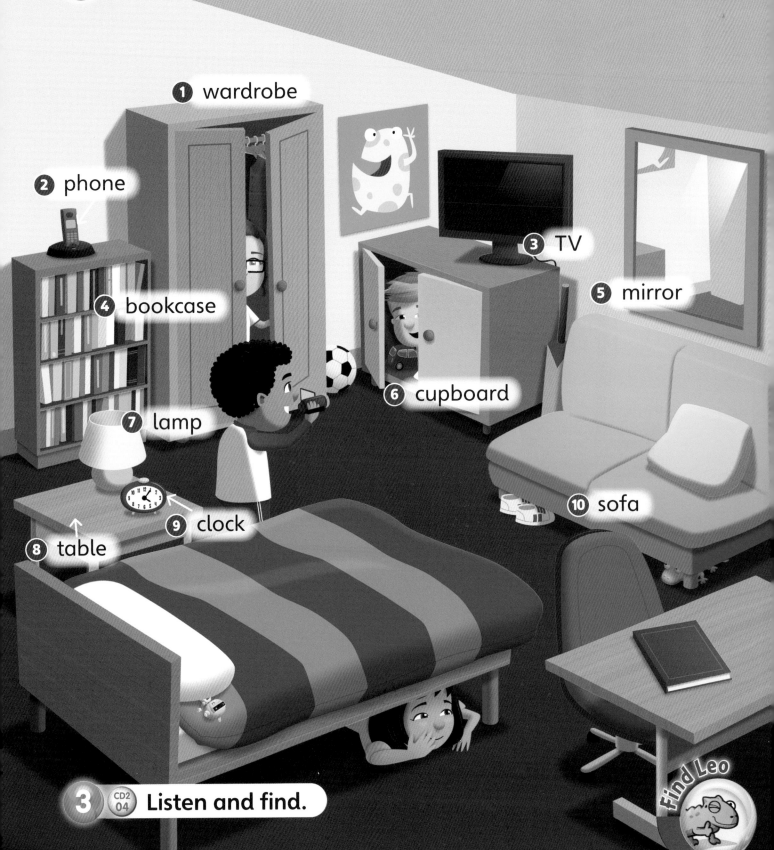

1 wardrobe

2 phone

3 TV

4 bookcase

5 mirror

6 cupboard

7 lamp

8 table

9 clock

10 sofa

Find Leo

3 (CD2 04) **Listen and find.**

Say the chant.

Is the lamp on the table?
Yes, it is. Yes, it is.
The lamp's on the table.

Are the books in the bookcase?
Yes, they are. Yes, they are.
The books are in the bookcase.

lamp

bookcase

clock

wardrobe

 Look, ask and answer.

Is the TV on the bookcase? No, it isn't. It's on the table.

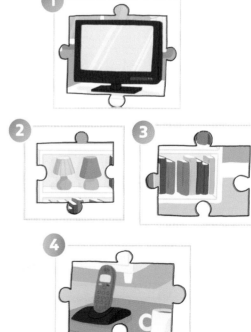

 What's in your bedroom? Think and say. My computer is on my desk.

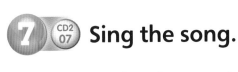

7 CD2 07 **Sing the song.**

It's moving day, it's moving day
And everything's wrong on
moving day.

There's a 🛋 in the bathroom.
There's a 🪑 in the hall.
There's a 🗄 in the kitchen.
And I can't find my ball!

It's moving day …

There are four 💡s in the garden.
There are two 🖼 s on my bed.
There are three 🕐s on the sofa.
And where is baby Fred?

It's moving day …

8 CD2 08 **Listen and say *yes* or *no*.**

9 CD2 09 Listen, look and say.

10 CD2 10 Listen, count and answer the questions.

How many fish are there?

Seventeen!

11 Think Play the game.

There are three spiders.   No!

12 🔊 CD2 11 Listen and read.

1 Oh no! Where's my ring?

Is it in the art set?

2 Look at this big bookcase!

There's my doll. We're in my bedroom!

PETS TRANSPORT

3 Let's go in. Walk on me!

Thanks, iPal.

4 What a mess!

Let's tidy up.

5 Let's put the toys in the cupboard.

Now it's tidy.

6 What has iPal got?

It's your ring, Tina!

52 Value: Be tidy

→ Activity Book page 42

13 CD2 13 Talk Time **Listen and act.**

Animal sounds

14 CD2 14 **Listen and say.**

Meerkats have got mouths. Newts have got noses.

How **many** are there?

1 (CD2 16) **Listen and say.**

lamppost

bus stop

letterbox

traffic light

2 **Watch the video.**

3 **Look and say the number.**

How many lampposts are there?

There are fourteen.

Guess What!

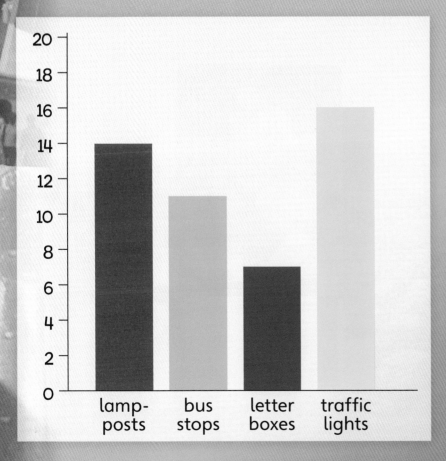

Project

4 Make a bar chart.

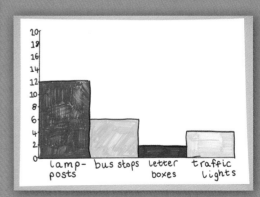

CLIL: Maths **55**

Review Units 3 and 4

1 Look and say the words. Number 1. Jeans.

2 CD2 17 Listen and say the colour.

3 Play the game.

Finish

Are you wearing a ? **17**

How many are there in your house? **18**

Are you wearing a 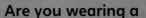 ? **19**

GO BACK ONE! **20**

MISS A TURN! **16**

How many  are there in your bathroom? **15**

Are you wearing a  ? **14**

How many  are there in your classroom? **13**

Are you wearing a  ? **9**

How many are there in your kitchen? **10**

Are you wearing  ? **11**

GO BACK ONE! **12**

GO FORWARD ONE! **8**

How many  are there in your living room? **7**

Are you wearing  ? **6**

How many  are there in your bedroom? **5**

Are you wearing  ? **1**

How many  are there in your classroom? **2**

Are you wearing a  ? **3**

MISS A TURN!

Start

57

5 Meals

Guess What!

Say the chant.

breakfast

Do you like toast for breakfast?
Do you like cereal, too?
Toast and cereal for breakfast?
Yum! Yes, I do.

lunch   dinner

 Read, look and say. What's missing?

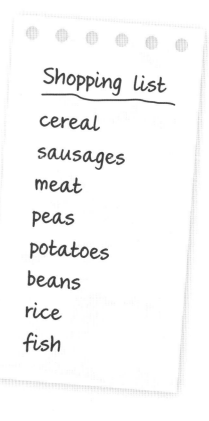

Shopping list

cereal
sausages
meat
peas
potatoes
beans
rice
fish

CD2 24 Sing the song.

My friend Sammy likes
 for lunch.
He doesn't like ,
And he doesn't like .
He likes and
And he likes .

Munch, Sammy.
Munch your lunch!

My friend Sally likes
for lunch.
She doesn't like ,
And she doesn't like .
She likes and
And and .

Munch, Sally.
Munch your lunch!

7 CD2 25 Listen and say *Sammy* or *Sally*.

8 About Me Ask and answer. Then say.

Do you like fish?

Yes, I do.

Alex likes fish.

9 CD2 27 **Listen, look and say.**

1

2

10 Think **Ask and answer.**

Tony

Tom

Is it a boy or a girl?

It's a boy.

Does he like meat?

Yes, he does.

Does he like carrots?

No, he doesn't.

It's Tony!

Kim

Pat

→ Activity Book page 51   Grammar: *Does he like cereal?* **63**

11 CD2 28 **Listen and read.**

1

Look! Café Hawaii!

Let's go for lunch!

2

Café Hawaii

Would you like fish and potatoes?

Yes, please!

No, thank you!

3

What about carrots or peas, iPal?

No, thank you!

4

Oh dear! What would you like, iPal?

Cake! I like chocolate cake.

5

More cake, please!

No, iPal. That's enough!

6

What's the matter?

He likes chocolate cake – a lot!

64 Value: Eat healthy food

→ Activity Book page 52

12   **Listen and act.**

Animal sounds

13 CD2 31 **Listen and say.**

A **s**eal in the **s**un. A **z**ebra in the **z**oo.

What type of **food** is it?

1 CD2 33 Listen and say.

fruit

vegetables

meat

grains

dairy

2 Watch the video.

3 Look and say what type of food it is.

Number 1. Fruit.   Yes.

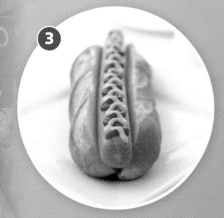

Guess What!

Project

4 Make a food poster.

fruit and vegetables   meat and fish   dairy   grains and cereals

Activities

Guess
What!

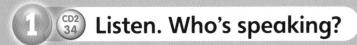

1 (CD2 34) **Listen. Who's speaking?**

2 (CD2 35) **Listen, point and say.**

Activity Day What can you do?

1. play tennis
2. play hockey
3. play basketball
4. rollerskate
5. play baseball
6. ride a horse
7. fly a kite
8. take photos

TODAY!

3 (CD2 36) **Listen and find.**

Find Leo

4 CD2 37 Say the chant.

I can play tennis.
I can't play hockey.
Let's play tennis.
Good idea!

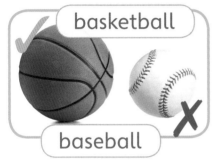

basketball
baseball

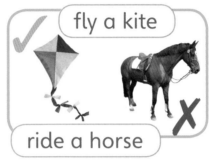

fly a kite
ride a horse

take photos
rollerskate

5 (About Me) Match and say.

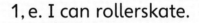 1, e. I can rollerskate.

1 I can rollerskate.
2 I can take photos.
3 I can ride a horse.
4 I can play tennis.
5 I can play hockey.

a

b

c

d

e

6 (About Me) Point and tell your friend.

Picture b. I can play tennis.   Picture e. I can't rollerskate.

→ Activity Book page 57   Vocabulary **71**

7 (CD2 39) Listen, look and say.

1 I like playing basketball, I don't like swimming.

2 I like swimming. I don't like playing basketball.

8 (CD2 40) Listen and say the name.

Ann

Pam

Jack

Bill

Alex

Grace

9 (About Me) Things you like. Think and say.

I like painting.   He likes painting.

10 CD2 41 Sing the song.

Do you like ✈?
No, I don't. No, I don't.
Do you like 🚲?
Yes, I do. Yes, I do.
I like 🚲!

Does he like ✈?
No, he doesn't. No, he doesn't.
Does he like 🚲?
Yes, he does. Yes, he does.
He likes 🚲!

Do you like 🎾?
No, I don't. No, I don't.
Do you like ⚽?
Yes, I do. Yes, I do.
I like ⚽!

Does she like 🎾?
No, she doesn't. No, she doesn't.
Does she like ⚽?
Yes, she does. Yes, she does.
She likes ⚽!

11 CD2 42 Think Listen and say the number.

Grammar: *Do you like flying a kite?* **73**

Value: Play nicely

→ Activity Book page 60

13   **Listen and act.**

Animal sounds

14 CD2 46 **Listen and say.**

A **c**amel with
a **c**amera.
A **k**angaroo
with a **k**ite.

What equipment do we need?

1 CD2 48 **Listen and say.**

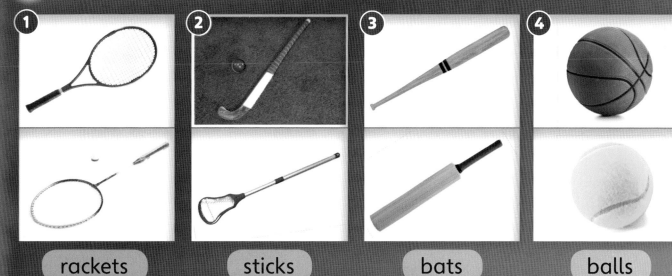

rackets   sticks   bats   balls

2 **Watch the video.**

3 **Look and say** *racket*, *stick*, *bat* or *ball*.

Number 1. Ball.   Yes!

Guess What!

Project

4 **Make a Carroll diagram.**

Review Units 5 and 6

 1 **Look and say the words.** Number 1. Fly a kite.

2 (CD2 49) **Listen and say the colour.**

Sue

Dan

→ Activity Book pages 64–65

3 Play the game.

7 In town

Guess What!

1 (CD3 02) **Listen. Who's speaking?**

2 (CD3 03) **Listen, point and say.**

1 park
2 cinema

CINEMA

Now Showing: **Robots From Outer Space**

4 café
5 toy shop
6 book shop
3 clothes shop
7 supermarket

ozy Café

The Toy Shop

Bert's Books

The Clothing Store

Supermarket

Beans
Coffee 30% Off
Fruit & Ve

8 street

SCHOOL

9 school

10 playground

Find Leo

3 (CD3 04) **Listen and find.**

→ Activity Book page 65

Say the chant.

sister

Come with me and look around.
Who's in the café in the town?
It's my sister! She's in the café.
She's in the café in the town.

brother

mum

dad

5 **Match and say.**

1, c. My cousin's in the playground.

1 My cousin's in the playground.
2 My aunt's in the clothes shop.
3 My uncle's in the school.
4 My grandma's in the supermarket.
5 My grandpa's in the park.

6 **Think of a place. Say and guess.**

There's a desk and green chairs.

It's a school.

7 (CD3 07) **Sing the song.**

Come and visit my town,
My friendly little town.
It's nice to be in my town,
My little town.

There's a toy shop and
    a clothes shop.
There's a book shop
    and a cinema.
There's a café and
    there's
a supermarket.
In my little town.

And the toy shop is behind the
    clothes shop.
And the book shop is in front of
    the clothes shop.
And the clothes shop is between
    the book shop and the toy shop!
In my little town.

And the cinema is next to the café.
And the café is next to the supermarket.
And the café is between the supermarket
    and the cinema.

Come and visit my town ...

8 (CD3 08) **Look, listen and find the mistakes.**

The cinema is next to the supermarket.

No it isn't. The cinema is next to the café.

9 **CD3 09** **Listen, look and say.**

Is there a playground behind the school?   Yes, there is.

Is there a café next to the cinema?   No, there isn't.

10 **CD3 10** **Listen and say *yes* or *no*.**

11 **Think** **Play the game.**

Is there a café in front of the supermarket?

Yes, there is.

The cinema is next to the school.

No, it isn't. The cinema is next to the supermarket.

1. Cinema tickets!
   They're from my cousin, Anna!

2. Where's the cinema?
   It's next to the supermarket.

3. Let's go!
   No, iPal! Be careful!

4. Look left and right.
   It's safe now. Let's cross.

5. Oh, no! It's closed today!
   Come with me!

6. It's a film about robots!
   I like going to the cinema.

13   **Listen and act.**

Animal sounds

14   **Listen and say.**

A quick queen bee. An ox with an x-ray.

Where are the
places?

1 (CD3 16) **Listen and say.**

police station   fire station   hospital   sports centre

2 Watch the video.

3 Look and say the letter and number.

A, 3.   Fire station.   Yes!

Guess What!

Project

4 Draw a map of your town.

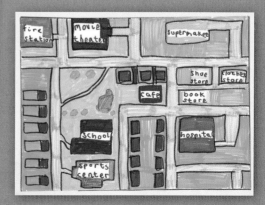

→ Activity Book page 72

8 On the farm

Guess What!

1 [CD3 17] Listen. Who's speaking?

2 [CD3 18] Listen, point and say.

1 field

2 barn

3 horse

Café and Gift Shop

4 donkey

5 sheep

6 goat

7 cow

8 duck

3 [CD3 19] Listen and find.

9 pond

Find Leo

4 CD3 20 Say the chant.

donkey

goats

Where's the donkey?
It's in the barn.
It's in the barn.
On the farm.

Where are the goats?
They're in the field.
They're in the field.
On the farm.

cow

ducks

5 Read and follow. Then ask and answer.

Where's the cow?   It's in the field.

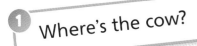
1 Where's the cow?

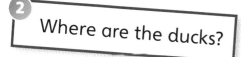
2 Where are the ducks?

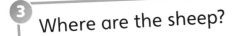
3 Where are the sheep?

4 Where's the horse?

a

b

c

6 (About Me) Ask and answer.

What's your favourite animal?   It's a sheep.

7 (CD3 22) **Sing the song.**

Field and pond, house and barn,
Look at the animals on the farm …

What's the doing?
It's swimming. It's swimming.
It's swimming
What's the doing?
It's swimming in the .

Field and pond …

What's the doing?
It's running. It's running. It's running
What's the doing?
It's running in the  .

Field and pond …

What's the  doing?
It's sleeping. It's sleeping.
It's sleeping
What's the  doing?
It's sleeping in the  .

Field and pond …

What's the  doing?
It's eating. It's eating. It's eating
What's the  doing?
It's eating in the  .

Field and pond …

8 (CD3 23) **Listen and answer the questions.**

What's the duck doing?   It's swimming.

1
2
3
4
5
6
7
8

94 Grammar: *What's the duck doing?*   → Activity Book page 76

9  **Listen, look and say.**

1   Is the cat sleeping?   Yes, it is.

2   Is the duck swimming?   No, it isn't. It's flying.

10 Think **Play the game.**

Is the dog running?

Yes, it is.

Picture 1!

Grammar: *Is the cat sleeping?* **95**

1. It's a message for iPal.
   Let's find him!

2. Would you like to come to a party?
   Yes, please!

3. Hold on!
   We're flying!

4. Welcome to the party!
   It's so nice to see you!
   WELCOME HOME iPAL

5. What's Ben doing?
   He's ... dancing!

6. Goodbye, iPal!
   Goodbye! Thanks for looking after me!

→ Activity Book page 78

12   **Listen and act.**

Animal sounds

13 (CD3 29) **Listen and say.**

A wolf in the water. A white whale with a wheel.

Functional language: *Would you like to come to my party?*
Pronunciation: *w, wh* **97**

What do
farmers do?

1 CD3 31 Listen and say.

plant seeds

turn soil

water plants

harvest plants

2 Watch the video.

3 Look and say.

Number 1. He turns the soil.   Yes!

Guess What!

Project

4 Draw how farmers grow our food.

Review   Units 7 and 8

1 Look and say the words.   Number 1. Café.

 1
 2
 3
 4

 5
 6
 7
 8

2 CD3 32 Listen and say the name.

Grace

Lola

Kento

Dan

3 Ask and answer.

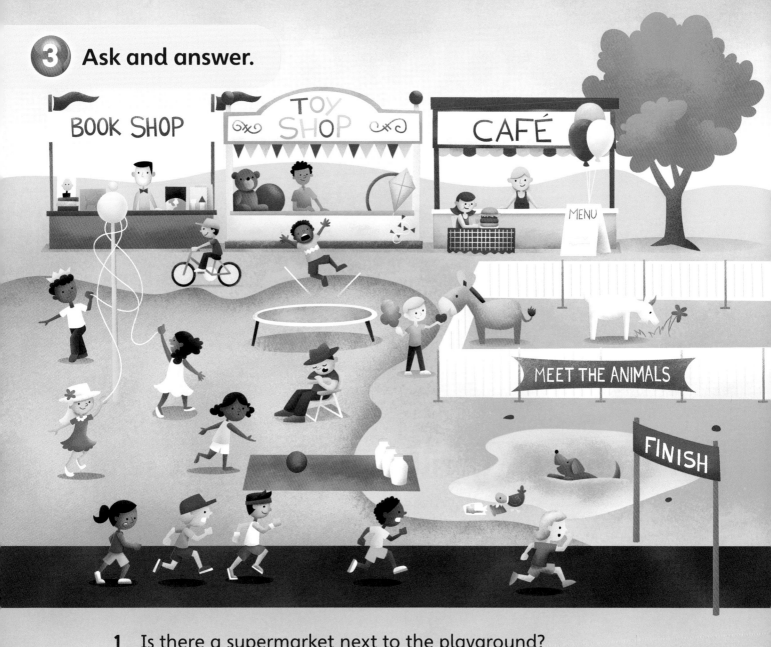

1 Is there a supermarket next to the playground?

2 What is between the book shop and the café?

3 Is there a pond in the park?

4 What is the duck doing?

5 Is the dog sleeping?

6 What is the donkey doing?

7 Is she eating cereal?

8 What's he doing?

9 Is she swimming?

10 What's he doing?

My sounds

lion • rabbit

gorilla • hippo

fox • vulture

jakal • yak

meerkat • newt

seal • zebra

camel • kangaroo

queen bee • ox

wolf • whale

Thanks and Acknowledgements

Many thanks to everyone in the excellent team at Cambridge University Press. In particular we would like to thank Emily Hird, Liane Grainger and Flavia Lamborghini whose professionalism, enthusiasm, experience and talent makes them all such a pleasure to work with.

We would also like to give special thanks to Lesley Koustaff for her unfailing support, expert guidance, good humour and welcome encouragement throughout the project.

The authors and publishers would like to thank the following contributors:

Blooberry Design: concept design, cover design, book design, page make-up
Emma Szlachta: editing
Ann Thomson: art direction, picture research
Gareth Boden: commissioned photography
Jon Barlow: commissioned photography
Ian Harker: audio recording
Robert Lee, Dib Dib Dub Studios: song and chant composition
Vince Cross: theme tune composition
James Richardson: arrangement of theme tune
Phaebus: video production

The authors and publishers acknowledge the following sources of copyright material and are grateful for the permissions granted. While every effort has been made, it has not always been possible to identify the sources of all the material used, or to trace all copyright holders.

If any omissions are brought to our notice, we will be happy to include the appropriate acknowledgements on reprinting.

The authors and publishers would like to thank the following illustrators:

Bill Bolton, pp41; Marek Jagucki, pp5, 6, 7, 10, 15, 16, 20, 25, 26, 30, 37, 38, 42, 47, 48, 52, 59, 60, 64, 69, 70, 74, 81, 82, 86, 91, 92, 96; Kirsten Collier (Bright Agency), pp11, 21, 31, 43, 53, 65, 75, 87, 97, 102, 103; Andy Parker, pp39, 89; Phil Garner (Beehive Illustration), pp17, 27; Joelle Dreidemy (Bright Agency), pp27, 61, 83; Woody Fox (Bright Agency), pp8, 18, 29, 40, 50, 62, 73, 84; Richard Watson (Bright Agency), pp28, 41, 51, 63, 95; Chris Jevons (Bright Agency), pp51; Marcus Cutler (Sylvie Poggio), pp35, 57, 79, 101; Gareth Conway, pp49

The authors and publishers would like to thank the following for permission to reproduce photographs:

p.2–3: Galyna Andrushko/shutterstock; p.4–5: Images Etc Ltd/Getty Images; p.8 (Dan): Valua Vitaly/Shutterstock; p.8 (Jill): Jacek Chabraszewski/Shutterstock; p.8 (Sam), p.34 (Bill): Monkey Business Images/Shutterstock; p.8 (Sue): Lorelyn Medina/Shutterstock; p.8 (Tom): michaeljung/Shutterstock; p.9 (CL): AnnaIA/Shutterstock; p.9 (C): terekhov igor/Shutterstock; p.9 (CR): Wil Tilroe-Otte/Shutterstock; p.9 (BL): Gena73/Shutterstock; p.9 (BC): incamerastock/Alamy; p.9 (BR): Mikhail Olykaynen/Alamy; p.11 (B/G), p.32 (B/G), p.43 (B/G), p.53 (B/G), p.75 (B/G): Tim Jackson/Getty Images; p.12: Robin Weaver/Alamy; p.13 (1): scyther5/Shutterstock; p.13 (2): Chukcha/Shutterstock; p.13 (3): veryan dale/Alamy; p.13 (4): Africa Studio/Shutterstock; p.13 (CL): Serge Vero/Shutterstock; p.13 (CR): Matej Kastelic/Shutterstock; p.13 (BL): Corbis; p.13 (BC): MaKars/Shutterstock; p.14–15: Guido Cozzi/Corbis; p.17 (1), p.17 (c), p.34 (3): Argentieri/Getty Images; p.17 (2), p.17 (d): James Steidl/Shutterstock; p.17 (3), p.17 (b): Margo Harrison/Shutterstock; p.17 (4), p.17 (a): John Orsbun/Shutterstock; p.19 (a): Scott Rothstein/Shutterstock; p.19 (b): V. J. Matthew/Shutterstock; p.19 (c): s oleg/Shutterstock; p.19 (d): Aprilphoto/Shutterstock; p.19 (e): Mikael Damkier/Shutterstock; p.21 (B/G): SZE FEI WONG/Getty Images; p.22–23: imageBROKER/Alamy; p.23 (TL): Buzz Pictures/Alamy; p.23 (TC): David Fowler/Shutterstock; p.23 (TR): Dwight Smith/Shutterstock; p.23 (CL): Bailey-Cooper Photographer/Alamy; p.23 (C): antb/Shutterstock; p.23 (CR): Dhoxax/Shutterstock; p.23 (1): Andrey Pavlov/Shutterstock; p.23 (2): Elena Elisseeva/Shutterstock; p.23 (3): Patrick Foto/Shutterstock; p.23 (4): maxpro/Shutterstock; p.24–25: antos777/Getty Images; p.27 (men): Viorel Sima/Shutterstock; p.27 (women): stockyimages/Shutterstock; p.27 (babies): StockLite/Shutterstock; p.27 (children): Gelpi JM/Shutterstock; p.32–33: SurangaSL/Shutterstock; p.33 (TL): Barna Tanko/Shutterstock; p.33 (TC): g215/Shutterstock; p.33 (TR): Tierfotoagentur/Alamy; p.33 (CL): J Reineke/Shutterstock; p.33 (C): skynetphoto/Shutterstock; p.33 (CR): Galyna Andrushko/Shutterstock; p.33 (2): Don Fink/Shutterstock; p.33 (2): David Sucsy/Getty Images; p.33 (3): BarbarosKARAGULMEZ/Getty Images; p.33 (4): Vitaly Titov & Maria Sidelnikova; p.34 (1): DWD-photo/Alamy; p.34 (2): shane partdridge/Alamy; p.34 (4): Mikael Damkier/Shutterstock; p.34 (5): paul prescott/Shutterstock; p.34 (6): Tsekhmister/Shutterstock; p.34 (7): Olga Bogatyrenko/Shutterstock; p.34 (8): DenisNata/Shutterstock; p.34 (Tony): MANDY GODBEHEAR/Shutterstock; p.34 (Anna): Judy Kennamer/Shutterstock; p.34 (May): Victoria Blackie/Getty Images; p.34 (BL): Willyam Bradberry/Shutterstock; p.34 (BC dog): Matthew Williams-Ellis/Shutterstock; p.34 (BC mice): Geoffrey Lawrence/

Shutterstock; p.34 (BR): DreamBig/Shutterstock; p.36–37: Bartosz Hadyniak/Getty Images; p.39 (TL): Mo Peerbacus/Alamy; p.39 (TR): artproem/Shutterstock; p.39 (CL): Zoonar GmbH/Alamy; p.39 (CR): Irina Rogova/Shutterstock; p.44–45: Tim Gainey/Alamy; p.45 (T-1): THPStock/Shutterstock; p.45 (T-2): Sofiaworld/Shutterstock; p.45 (T-3): smereka/Shutterstock; p.45 (T-4): Randy Rimland/Shutterstock; p.45 (cotton): pixbox77/Shutterstock; p.45 (silk): Tramont_ana/Shutterstock; p.45 (leather): Illustrar L/Shutterstock; p.45 (wool): trossofoto/Shutterstock; p.45 (B-1): Lucy Liu/Shutterstock; p.45 (B-2): Picsfive/Shutterstock; p.45 (B-3): karkas/Shutterstock; p.45 (B-4): Gulgun Ozaktas/Shutterstock; p.45 (B-5): Loskutnikov/Shutterstock; p.46–47: LeeYiuTung/Getty Images; p.49 (TL): LianeM/Getty Images; p.49 (TR): donatas1205/Shutterstock; p.49 (CL): akud/Shutterstock; p.49 (CR), p.56 (8), p.56 (CL): Image Source/Alamy; p.53 (TR): Datacraft – QxQ images/Alamy; p.54–55, p.89 (3): Justin Kase zsixz/Alamy; p.55 (1): Radius Images/Alamy; p.55 (2): Taina Sohlman/Shutterstock; p.55 (3): ATGImages/Shutterstock; p.55 (4): stocker1970/Shutterstock; p.56 (1): Teerasak/Shutterstock; p.56 (2): Kitch Bain/Shutterstock; p.56 (3): Marek Uszynski/Shutterstock; p.56 (4): Pearlimage/Alamy; p.56 (5): Africa Studio/Shutterstock; p.56 (6): Chukcha/Shutterstock; p.56 (7): Nolte Lourens/Shutterstock; p.56 (BL): Bart Broek/Getty Images; p.58–59: Naho Yoshizawa/Shutterstock; p.63 (Tony): Craig Richardson/Alamy5; p.63 (Kim): Tracy Whiteside/Alamy; p.63 (Tom): Blend Images/Alamy; p.63 (Pat): Tracy Whiteside/Alamy; p.63 (meat): Jacek Chabraszewski/Shutterstock; p.63 (fish): Eskymaks/Shutterstock; p.63 (potatoes): Kevin Mayer/Shutterstock; p.63 (carrots): Maria Komar/Shutterstock; p.63 (rice): oriori/Shutterstock; p.63 (beans): mayer kleinostheim/Shutterstock; p.63 (toast): alnavegante/Shutterstock; p.65 (B/G), p.97 (B/G): Jolanta Wojcicka/Shutterstock; p.65 (T): Andrew Olney/Shutterstock; p.66–67: Stefano Politi Markovina/Alamy; p.67 (T-1): matka_Wariatka/Shutterstock; p.67 (T-2): sarsmis/Shutterstock; p.67 (T-3): Jag_cz/Shutterstock; p.67 (T-4): Christine Langer-Pueschel/Shutterstock; p.67 (T-5): Christian Draghici/Shutterstock; p.67 (B-1): koss13/Shutterstock; p.67 (B-2): Christian Jung/Shutterstock; p.67 (B-3): Adam Gault/Getty Images; p.67 (B-4): Africa Studio/Shutterstock; p.68–69: Leander Baerenz/Getty Images; p.71 (baseball): Dan Thornberg/Shutterstock; p.71 (basketball): Aaron Amat/Shutterstock; p.71 (kite): Hurst Photo/Shutterstock; p.71 (horse): Alex White/Shutterstock; p.71 (camera): taelove7/Shutterstock; p.71 (skates), p.71 (e): J. Helgason/Shutterstock; p.71 (a): gorillaimages/Shutterstock; p.71 (b): Veronica Louro/Shutterstock; p.71 (c): Ramona Heim/Shutterstock; p.71 (d): Rob Bouwman/Shutterstock; p.72 (C): Hybrid Images/Getty Images; p.72 (CR): Production Perig/Shutterstock; p.72 (CL): racorn/Shutterstock; p.72 (BL): auremar/Shutterstock; p.72 (BR): Kuttig - People/Alamy; p.75 (T): F1online digitale Bildagentur GmbH/Alamy; p.76–77: 13/David Madison/Ocean/Corbis; p.77 (T-1); p.77 (T-2): Image Source Plus/Alamy; p.77 (T-3): onilmilk/Shutterstock; p.77 (T-4): Aaron Amat/Shutterstock; p.77 (rackets): anaken2012/Shutterstock; p.77 (sticks): Bill Frische/Shutterstock; p.77 (bats): Sean Gladwell/Shutterstock; p.77 (balls): mexrix/Shutterstock; p.77 (B-1): Pal2iyawit/Shutterstock; p.77 (B-2): Ian Buchan/Shutterstock; p.77 (B-3): isitsharp/Getty Images; p.77 (B-4): Visionhaus/Corbis; p.78 (1): Fir4ik/Shutterstock; p.78 (2): Ledo/Shutterstock; p.78 (3): Nattika/Shutterstock; p.78 (4): Ramon grosso dolarea/Shutterstock; p.78 (5): Tischenko Irina/Shutterstock; p.78 (6): igor.stevanovic/Shutterstock; p.78 (7): Joe Gough/Shutterstock; p.78 (8): Elnur/Shutterstock; p.78 (Sue): Tracy Whiteside/Shutterstock; p.78 (Dan): oliveromg/Shutterstock; p.78 (BC skates): StockPhotosArt/Shutterstock; p.78 (BC hockey): Leonid Shcheglov/Shutterstock; p.78 (BL): Igor Dutina/Shutterstock; p.78 (BR): Lauri Patterson/Getty Images; p.80–81: Peter Burnett/Getty Images; p.83 (TL): Gladskikh Tatiana/Shutterstock; p.83 (brother): Pavel L Photo and Video/Shutterstock; p.83 (mum): racorn/Shutterstock; p.83 (dad): Carlos Yudica/Shutterstock; p.87 (B/G): Brett Baunton/Alamy; p.87 (T): Adrian Sherratt/Alamy; p.88: A.P.S.(UK)/Alamy; p.89 (1): T.M.O.Buildings/Alamy; p.89 (2): Andrew Paterson/Alamy; p.89 (4): Mike Robinson/Alamy; p.90–91: Getty Images; p.93 (TL): Dieter Hawlan/Shutterstock; p.93 (TR): Orhan Cam/Shutterstock; p.93 (CL): Sebastian Knight/Shutterstock; p.93 (CR): Isantilli/Shutterstock; p.93 (a): American Spirit/Shutterstock; p.93 (b): Scott Prokop/Shutterstock; p.93 (c): Brian Goodman/Shutterstock; p.94 (B/G): Dudarev Mikhail/Shutterstock; p.94 (horse): Lenkadan/Shutterstock; p.94 (field): robert_s/Shutterstock; p.94 (duck): Geanina Bechea/Shutterstock; p.94 (pond): Yuriy Kulik/Shutterstock; p.94 (cat): Rumo/Shutterstock; p.94 (house): bbofdon/Shutterstock; p.94 (cow): jesadaphorn/Shutterstock; p.94 (barn): Bonita R. Cheshier/Shutterstock; p.94 (1): Diane Picard/Shutterstock; p.94 (2): Schubbel/Shutterstock; p.94 (3): Ewa Studio/Shutterstock; p.94 (4): Michael Durham/Getty Images; p.94 (5): Makarova Viktoria/Shutterstock; p.94 (6): Kemeo/Shutterstock; p.94 (7): Ballawless/Shutterstock; p.94 (8): Alexander Matvienko/Alamy; p.98–99: Stephen Dorey/Getty Images; p.99 (1): Danylo Saniylenko/Shutterstock; p.99 (2): Tim Scrivener/Alamy; p.99 (3): Keith Dannemiller/Corbis; p.99 (4): Alex Treadway/National Geographic Society/Corbis; p.100 (1): Shchipkova Elena/Shutterstock; p100 (2): Arterra Picture Library/Alamy; p.100 (3): THPStock/Shutterstock; p.100 (4): Brandon Seidel/Shutterstock; p.100 (5): 1stGallery/Shutterstock; p.100 (6): Denise Lett/Shutterstock; p.100 (7): imageBROKER/Alamy; p.100 (8): IxMaster/Shutterstock; p.100 (CL): Blend Images/Alamy; p.100 (CR), p.100 (BR): imageBROKER/Alamy; p.100 (BL): Alinute Silzeviciute/Shutterstock.

Commissioned photography by Gareth Boden: p.13 (BR), p.23 (BR), p.33 (BR), p.45 (BR), p.55 (BR), p.67 (BR), p.77 (BR), p.89 (BR), p.99 (BR); Jon Barlow: p.9 (T), p.11 (T), p.19 (T), p.19 (C), p.21 (T), p.28, p.31 (T), p.41 (T), p.43 (T), p.56 (CR), p.56 (BR), p.61, p.62, p.71 (T), p.72 (TL), p.72 (TR), p.72 (BC), p.85, p.95 (B), p. 97 (T).

Our special thanks to the following for their kind help during location photography:

Everyone Active-Parkside Pool Cambridge, Queen Emma Primary School

Front Cover photo by Lynne Gilbert/Getty Images